Carnival

Adam Taylor

First published 2022
Crosswave Publishing

ISBN 978-0-9565561-7-2

With thanks to Jeff Vinter and Stephen Bishop
Cover illustration *Earth Angel* by Lynne Fornieles
Designed by Jeff Vinter

Set in Book Antiqua

Printed in Great Britain by ImprintDigital.com
Imprint Academic Ltd, Unit 1, Seychelles Farm, Upton Pyne, Devon, EX5 5HY

To Cristina

Introduction

Originally, Carnival was the period of feasting and revelry before the penitential season of Lent, which precedes Easter. The word is an abbreviation of the phrase *carnem levare,* that is, 'to remove meat' – meat which could not be eaten during Lent; but a popular etymology derived the word from *carne vale,* 'Flesh, farewell!'

Adam Taylor
Chichester. 2022

Contents

I

Waking in Weymouth

5 a.m. A tractor tows a rake,
inscribing perfect arcs along the shore,
then – surely more for Art than Hygiene's sake –
around the swings, canoes and deckchair-store
a casual, practised, undulating wake.

In painted effigy, King George surveys
the first excited dog to print the sand
and a first, restless tourist, come to gaze
(an architectural guidebook in his hand)
at the vacant Esplanade. Its buildings raise

pale faces to the sun as if reborn
to air that's microscopically clear.
Such pristine pavements! Are they swept at dawn?
Does paper vanish, glass not shatter here?
Or has some glittering flood just now withdrawn?

Plainly, someone cares about this place –
cares, too, about the visitors, to whom
the bay extends a catholic embrace.
No-one shall linger coffined in his room,
no tear flow unconsoled. Beard every face

with candy-floss! Let the old reveal
marmoreal limbs or link arms in pubs,
grandchildren ride the carousel or squeal
at Punch and Judy, the young gyrate in clubs,
coining lubricious glances! And may it heal –

may this town heal us. May we wake to see
cash and class powerless to divide us,
learn to forget ourselves a while and, free
from landlocked Worry, with the sea beside us,
make our daily patterns gracefully.

The Neighbour
after Rilke

Why follow me, strange violin?
I've barely started to unpack
when you strike up beyond the thin
hotel-partition at my back.

Your owner's talents ought to find
an audience quite readily;
the suicidally-inclined
are numerous. Why pick on me?

And why must my neighbour's repertory
consist in coaxing from your strings
a tune that tells the same old story:
'Life is hardest of all hard things'?

Camera Obscura

Waking alone, no longer young,
he tried to focus on a face,
a lucid blur, tumbled among
the debris of a time and place:

Bloomsbury, in seventy-two.
And there he was, hirsute, great-coated,
loping toward their *rendezvous,*
the corner café, where they floated

at smeared tables, over stewed tea,
through lunch-breaks vague with noise and smoke,
she flushed with cold and bright-eyed, he
so sick with love he hardly spoke.

How sharply it came back, that first
winter away from home, the sense
of childish certainties dispersed
by every new experience

in vertiginous drifts like pigeons!
The bookshop where she worked between
erotica and odd religions;
cheap seats, tilted beneath the screen

at film seasons in Japanese;
the parties they endured together,
adrift among the coteries,
the boys in flowers, girls in leather;

the bedsit up four flights of stairs
where he mislaid virginity;
the tramps in the snow-dusted squares;
he saw them with such clarity,

why did her face remain a blur?
Or … no, not blurred … It was as if
the desire he still felt for her
dazzled memory, or as if …

The winter sun …
It filled the end of Coptic Street,
blazing in every crystal on
the frost-bound pavement at his feet

and she, against it, seemed to glow
like a blown coal, now bright, now dim,
consumed by the same fire that, though
less fiercely now, still quickened him.

Port Cupid

Dragging suitcases as heavy as bodies, we slithered by windlight
down lanes of irregular paving that villagers' bare feet had polished.
Taverns spilled snatches of music. Arches gave onto nothing.
Stairs wandered off in the dark and from somewhere beneath us
rose the clammy breath of a giant in the toils of a nightmare.
Too late! Plainly, we'd left our escape to the south too late:
money had migrated; shop-girls were blanching in grey northern cities;
fishermen's randy sons had glumly returned to netting
fish, not mermaids, and we were condemned to a fortnight's confinement
in a damp cupboard with Proust and Jane Austen.
                                        Next morning, however,
we woke to a tiger of sunlight. I crossed the cool floor-tiles, wrenched open
flaky green shutters and – Oh, look! There was the bay, its surface
barely ruffled; and, curled on its floor in pyjama-less slumber,
lay last night's giant, no more than a boy, peacefully dreaming
while yachts, paper-frail, scudded above him. Of course, we must have one.
We hired it from a gorilla (sailor, alas, no longer!)
at the quay where Maddalena, her face half classical beauty,
half mulberry tallow, sat in her booth telling fishermen's fortunes.
I eyed his cockleshell, he my sea-legs, with equal suspicion;

then, closing his creased palm on my obol, he passed me a
    frayed rope
at which a tub with knotted rigging and scrofulous varnish
tugged like a puppy. Leaving the village, flapping with
    laundry,
we scraped, in lubberly fashion, the guardian rocks of the
    harbour,
whence the giant thrust us toward a small patch of yellow
far over the water where, surely, elusive Happiness waited.

It was on our return from that beach (which proved stony,
    crowded and littered)
that trouble began. The mainstay parted and when we'd
    repaired it
what breeze there was breathed its last. Small waves jostled
    our dinghy
round which our recriminations spread in an ominous
    silence
as if someone were listening – not understanding, but
    listening.
Only when we had reached – we hardly knew how – the
    harbour
did we notice the ugly bruise that disfigured the sky behind
    us.
On terrace and balcony, women in black were bringing in
    washing.
The gorilla sat moaning, his head in his hands, and of
    Maddalena
nothing remained but a single card by our mooring: the
    Hanged Man.
We pulled the door shut as the first, fat drops spattered the
    paving.

Gutters spawned quicksilver and dust-choked downpipes
    chuckled
as, chilled and exhausted, we curled up in bed and, above
    us, the giant
beat with fists of air on the pantiles in impotent anger.
How glad we were to lie in our warmth while he was
    excluded!
But our dreams betrayed us; they lifted the latch at his
    summons.
Through empty streets, in a grey twilight, we picked our
    way barefoot
down to the quay and boarded the dinghy waiting there for
    us.
The sails filled and we skimmed across the seething black
    water
till the giant, weary of playing, reached out a plump arm
    and idly
smashed our boat and limp bodies against the sharp rocks
    of the harbour.

A Photograph

You'd imagine, hearing her talk,
the place were a lifetime away:
that deserted half-moon of a bay
where red sandstone fades into chalk.

She shows me the creased photograph –
shows it without letting go –
and when I assure her I know
that coastline replies with a laugh:

'You won't have found my bay, I'm sure.
I was brought up – well, grew up – nearby,
running wild between water and sky
till Father left, slamming the door,

and Mother came up with a scheme
for a dazzling career as a singer.
No argument I knew could bring her
to abandon pursuit of her dream.

We were bankrupt in less than a year.
The house went for auction and, fool
that I was, I dropped out of school
at fifteen – and ended up here.'

Would she ever return? 'One day,
perhaps – I just might – in a hearse'.
She opens an orderly purse
and slips her lost childhood away.

'A bit far for a funeral parade?'
She smiles and returns to her work –
the work she does well, the dull work
which ensures that her mortgage is paid.

Of course, I've no licence to preach;
I, too, try to keep life apart
from dreaming and practise the art
of putting my dreams out of reach –

the art which holds every device
legitimate if it mislead,
which falsifies maps and lets weed
and sapling reclaim paradise.

Endymion, or a Moonlit Letter

That tarnished obol, still exchanged between
the chaste and the inconstant, shines tonight
on the desk at which I sit up late to write,
on quiet houses and quiet street below,
silvering indifferently
the rubbish-bin, the pavement and the green
of grass and hedge, as wind silvers a willow
or raises spindrift on a slate-grey sea.

The traffic sleeps and, far beyond its breathing,
it's waves I hear, unclenching in the bay
where, in the sun's all-seeing gaze, we lay
alone, before the tourist season started,
Why was it that the unseasonably warm weather
cast such a shadow over me? What seething
dissatisfaction made me so hard-hearted
on that last holiday we took together?

Whatever it was, it drove me up the hill
toward the ruins of the Moorish fort,
while, to our bungalow, its obverse brought
Endymion, the gardener, a lad
whose vitals love was burning through,
sapping his youthful strength and modest skill,
and who, in the dozen English words he had,
poured out his doleful history to you.

And, yes, alright, I shouldn't have extended
his English lexicon and split his lip;
I found him in your arms and lost my grip –
or so I said. And now? Now, I confess:
his gentleness aroused my violence.
Endymion left in tears and something ended.

You said I couldn't love, only possess.
We slept apart and ate our meals in silence.

Soon after our return, we separated;
you went north to Edinburgh and I
here, to this Paris suburb. Months went by
in which our flat stood empty, its bare shelves
warped by the books we'd had to move.
We couldn't keep the place, but hesitated
to sell it, as if no-one but ourselves
should enter the small haven of our love.

Mare Vaporum, the Sea of Vapour,
Mare Frigoris, the Frozen Sea,
Mare Anguis, Sea of Jealousy –
I've waded in them all. Endymion
made me a votary of the moon,
condemned to fill sheet after sheet of paper
in trying to recapture what has gone.
I know I need to post this letter soon.

The Headland Cemetery
after Paul Valéry

Doves strut on the great roof that, tiled with waves,
shimmers between the pines, between the graves.
The midday sun tips each small crest with fire.
The sea, the sea, invents itself afresh;
and I, who struggled so long in its mesh,
float free into a calm beyond desire.

What host of aerial labourers is set
clambering Day's bright scaffolding, and yet
with what unconscious ease their work is done
when the sun seems, at its apogee, to pause
and raise from the abyss, like a first cause,
a fabric in which will and act are one.

Shrine sacred to Minerva, she whose treasure
is wisdom and whose blessings know no measure,
unsparing water, eye whose fathoms hold
dim, shelving dreams beneath a dazzling vesture,
your depths are mine and my soul's architecture
sustains this glittering roof, these tiles of gold.

To this high temple, in a breath erected,
that holds in every brick a sun reflected,
to this, my own Acropolis, I climb
from my home town to offer with the sea
the gift Creation gives Eternity:
the fragmentary brilliance of time.

How easily the boundary is crossed!
As easily as fruit, its contours lost,
is re-born on the palate as sensation,
so things become ideas and ideas things
and, like a greater sea, creation sings
the psalm of an unending transformation.

Unchanging Sky, look down on one whom change
gnaws like a chronic illness, whom a strange
passivity immured in his own head –
until today; today, an impulse sweeps me
beyond myself; only my shadow keeps me
tethered to the hovels of the dead.

Hatless in the purifying glare,
I own the justice of your searching stare.
O southern Sun, look down on what you made,
on me, to whom this littoral gave birth,
and see yourself reflected! Ah, but, on earth,
wherever there is light, there must be shade.

Not only works of art, but our lives, too,
must be informed by darkness to ring true.
Like a child on a clifftop tossing gravel
down some deep shaft, I listen as I write
for the distant echo of that inner night,
from which I issued and toward which travel.

But you, Water, behind the stooped pines trailing
your sequined coat or, through a rusted railing,
assailing tired eyes with your swarming brightness,
how can you know what torpor drags me back?
– the brain so dull, the body like a sack.
O, lend me just one spangle of your lightness!

This place apart where mortal flesh, returning
to nothingness, resolves in smokeless burning,
is solace and a balm to me; restored,
amid cracked marble and scorched flowers I stand
on this, the town's last tenancy of land
demised to death, this dragon-guarded hoard.

Sea-dragon, scaled with mirrors, keep away
all other living creatures; let me stay
alone here, pasturing my tranquil sheep,
my flock of graves; scare off the screaming
seabirds; let nothing interrupt the dreaming
of these provincial townsfolk; let them sleep.

There is no future here, no ticking clock,
only the cricket, fiddling on his rock.
Time here is loss, where sun and earth unknit
what once they made and from the rich
vintage of days distil an absence which
intoxicates Life with its opposite.

From skin and bone, you plait yourself a crown,
settle it on your head and hunker down
to rule unchallenged for a million years.
Sufficient to yourself and self-sustaining,
King Sun, above your worldly empire reigning
in me alone, your fool, you see your fears.

The doubts you cannot entertain, I know.
The pain you cannot feel, I undergo:
I am the dark spot wintering in your head.
But these, whose bodies leach between gnarled roots
and under crooked stones, are your recruits,
conscripted to the army of the dead.

They've melted and dissolved in earth,
ingested by the womb that gave them birth
and now confers their life on flowers. Where,
where are they now, the witty turn of phrase,
the skin softer than silk, the liquid gaze?
Parchment the face; worm-filled its vacant stare!

The grove gives birth to dryads; they, pursued
by stray gods, feel their limbs return to wood;
the endless chase continues, round and round.
What is desire but longing to escape
our brief imprisonment in human shape,
a longing soon requited underground?

What does it mean to say: 'After I die',
to claim a painted kingdom in the sky?
This globe of earth and water is our home;
we rise like waves and, driven toward land,
unfold at last our treasures on the sand
– a lifetime of experience lost in foam!

The slumber of the grave! Eternal rest!
What bitter milk it holds, the shrivelled breast
of Mother Nature, calling her children in!
These images of peace are a mere ruse;
who wouldn't, were he offered it, refuse
Death's true likeness: the fixed and mirthless grin?

Deep thinkers all, you who make your beds
like drunkards on the earth, whose empty heads
and thigh-bones raise the soil and catch our feet,
you cannot know the sharp-toothed worms that batten
on us, still upright in the room; they fatten
on us; it's only living flesh they eat.

To them, these parasites, our lives belong;
we gratify them, be we weak or strong.
Desire, regret, ambition, resignation,
self-love, self-hatred, name them as we will,
they are our close companions until
we leave them to another generation.

Zeno, old Greek, your paradoxes prove
that neither Death's feet nor his shaft can move:
Hector stays – once given a head-start –
beyond Achilles' grasp; the arrow stalls
in mid-trajectory and never falls.
Old Greek, your arrow has transfixed my heart.

What use, indeed, philosophy when Time
drags thinkers down, however high they climb?
I'm suffocating in this caul of thought;
I need to feel the sea-wind, salt and fresh,
expand my lungs, surf batter my flesh,
and know at what price consciousness is bought.

Creator and Destroyer, since my days
must finish in your maw, I'll sing your praise.
Praise, world-encircling dragon, be to you
whose ceaseless uproar is a kind of silence
and who, self-born and self-consumed in violence,
are alpha and omega, writ in blue!

Fly, dazzled pages! Flock of words, take wing
and, far from me, find ears in which to sing!
The wind awakes and claps my notebook shut.
The spell is broken; rise now, breakers, lash
this grave-encumbered promontory and smash
the great roof on which white sails peck and strut!

L'Étincelle (The Spark)
For Nick

We shared a parenthetic state,
like travellers in a railway carriage
(you fleeing England, I, a marriage)
and soon, by dint of talking late,
became night-owls. We'd quit our perch
as Paris lit up at our feet
and wing through the blue dusk in search
of somewhere cheap to drink and eat.

Baudelaire claims: *Nous avons dit*
souvent d'impérissables choses;
well, so did we – though heaven knows
quite what they were. At two or three,
the jazz clubs closed and we emerged
to join the dubious clientèle
which spent the hours till dawn submerged
in an all-night bar called *L'Étincelle.*

I see us through Time's telescope:
two homing specks, crossing as one
the red disk of the rising sun.
Young men in age, mere boys in hope,
we're chattering about … about …
jazz, girls, poetical careers,
and other riches stored, no doubt,
in the leaking treasury of years.

Miss Butterfly

'Some girls choose only once and she chose me.
Just twenty-one, she'd come ostensibly
to study English, in fact on an adventure
beyond the limits of her ordered world.
She was, like every Japanese I've known,
homesick on arrival for Japan;
you only have to live there for a while
for other countries to seem barbarous.
An older Englishman who spoke her language
piquantly combined known and unknown.
I teased her English, she, my Japanese;
and, soon, she stayed the night. When friends came round,
I'd sit and talk; she never joined us
except to serve plates of exquisite food.
Like all her nation, she worshipped a clean room;
the squalor of my little house appalled her.
She never criticised, of course; I'd wake to find
her place beside me vacant and, downstairs,
the kitchen spotless, flowers on the table.
She gained from me an idiomatic English
in which, when finally summoned home, she wrote,
forming the letters stroke by stroke, like *kanji*.
When next the currents that have ruled my life
returned me to Japan, I took a flat
an hour or so by train from where she lived.
She'd come at weekends, cook and tidy up,
but never stay more than a night or two,
in part, for form's sake – though her parents knew –
in part, not to disturb my solitude –
the solitude that was my habitat,
in which I read and tried to write a book,
a book that grew, but never found a shape.
I loved my small flat at the city edge,

traversed by sunlight, like a forest pool,
my library, ceramics and the view
of clouds snagged on the pines of *Daimonji*.

Years passed and, finally, since I said nothing,
blushing, with eyes downcast, she mentioned marriage.
What could I say? That the mere thought of drudging
to pay the rent and feed a family,
of pram-obstructed halls, filled me with dread?
I told her, falsely, I doubted I'd be faithful
and let her end our seven-year *affaire*.
Or almost end it: we met, at her suggestion,
one last time and I, though knowing better,
I turned up late. Lateness in Japan
is more than bad form; it offends against
their basic rule of mutual respect.
We reminisced and smiled – and knew for sure
we'd never meet again. When next I heard,
a matchmaker had found a husband for her –
a husband for a woman with a past.

Now here's a detail you might use in a poem.
I had a taste for glass – a western taste
for clarity; the Japanese prefer
clay vessels – unrevealing, self-contained.
That one is survivor of a pair
of Venetian goblets she gave me for a birthday.
The earthquake that struck Kobe shook my flat,
but nothing fell except the other goblet,
fell and smashed into a thousand fragments,
leaving its twin still upright on the shelf.'

I looked – he didn't – at the glaucous glass,
that might almost have been blown from sea-water
and stood a little out of true as if
inclined in grief toward its missing partner,
and thought about the shapes our lives had taken,
the hidden forces our frailty reveals.

Einsamkeit (Loneliness)

After Rilke

Loneliness resembles rain:
as vapour, it ascends
from dripping wood and sodden plain
to a children's party that always ends
with slamming doors and tears. Listen!
Thunder! Drops touch your window-pane;
slates are varnished, pavements glisten.

It rains in that uncertain hour
when, lost between the sun and moon,
blind alleys turn toward the dawn,
when couples, side by side in bed,
breathe like lungs. The party-goer,
meandering home with throbbing head,
is glad to feel the freshness. Soon,
in dusty gutters, runnels spawn,
autumn brings the curtain down
on a long summer and the town
is washed to innocence again.
Loneliness resembles rain.

O, Little Town

It's Christmas and, as if against my will,
I've returned to my native town,
freezing on its Kentish hillside
beneath stars too numerous to guide me.
I've travelled farther in time than space
down the passage that curves between two mirrors
toward the locked, aboriginal cupboard
where naked appetites debate
the source of impulse.
It's Christmas and I've returned
to the place I shall always call 'home'.

My father comes outside to greet us.
The children rush indoors to greet the dog
which, grey-muzzled and cloudy-eyed, wags
    acknowledgement.
The car is unpacked, the sherry drunk
in the over-heated drawing-room
and already I'm longing for air.
'He won't walk far, these days',
my father tells me, as I fasten the lead
and step, with a glad shock, into the cold,
the dog shambling behind me.
Well, I don't mean to go far –
not in space, at least.

The dog sniffs and I sniff;
the trail is still warm.
I follow the child I was along the 'Switchback'
to the meadow where he used to drag his sled,
the meadow that's like a socket,
in which the glittering constellations turn.
We climb the hill to the church and school.
I'm much too late for school and the gate has shrunk;

I'll never squeeze through now.
We pass the almshouse; thence
the deserted High Street leads us home.

'Yet in thy dark streets shineth'…
A Christmas tree blinks on and off
in the ironmonger's window.
There's not a soul abroad.
How little happens here!
One might die here, perhaps, but never, surely, be born.
Still along the London Road the lamps
form a question mark:
'Will you leave?', they asked my adolescent self. 'Can you?'
I thought I knew the answer, but, now?
It's Christmas and, as if against my will …

'Well, children, what can we give Him?'
I'm neither shepherd, nor wise man;
in whatever drama is performed here, I have no part;
and, yet, I return, as if to be counted,
when no-one should come empty-handed.
'What can we give Him, children?',
asks my Sunday-school teacher.
I shall give Him this bottle,
on the frosty pavement, still containing
the dregs drunkards leave as an oblation;
I shall give him this almost empty bottle
and say: 'This is my childhood
for which I am truly grateful,
its last, freezing drops of moonshine'.

Night-Fishers

They might almost be bushes, boulders,
they sit so still.
Night floods the meadow at their shoulders,
brims the canal, and renders rod and line
invisible.

Traffic on the by-pass sighs
as if asleep.
A mallard claps derisively and flies.
Cows rip the grass. Its being chosen makes
the silence deep.

The rooms that penned them flicker in
a garish light;
eyes stare at screens; ears buzz with din;
the mirror that enchants these fishermen
is lost to sight.

Upon it, jobs, debts, children, wives
leave not a mark;
its stillness underlies their lives
and raises wordless thoughts, as shy as fish,
out of the dark.

Alice

Inspiration pedals by
blue-stockinged on a bicycle.
Spire and tower pierce blue sky –
summer again; my thoughts are full
of you, of you. At once, the shaven grass
slips into shade. I gaze across
the chessboard through the looking glass

and see, on a white, distant square,
you, as a schoolgirl, walking home
through meadows to the old house where
light inundates your cluttered room.
But, oh!, between us days and nights stretch out
as, stumbling after you, I taste
the mortal wafer in my mouth.

Here, where adulthood confined me
with my moon-struck menagerie,
if Time allowed return, you'd find me
much the same. I've taken tea
with other girls, I don't deny, but then
you chose to age, my dear; you let
the glass freeze over me again.

Anniversary

My father died this day last year;
I suddenly remember
while walking down a London street
one grey day in November.

I miss, of course, his erudite,
good-humoured company;
but, more than that, I feel as if
a building, say, or tree,

some large, familiar, sheltering presence
that surely should be there
had disappeared. There is a new
discomfort in the air.

Reconciliation in Edinburgh

On the long road to the Far North of sleep,
I drift through Edinburgh in a willed dream,
climbing, like smoke from Waverley, some steep,
medieval close toward St Giles, eliding
High Street and Castlehill to fish the stream
of cloud for sunlight on the castle rampart
or, easily as any phantom, gliding
into the small, stone chapel at its heart.

It holds an antique mirror to the mind,
this city cloven into hemispheres –
Old Town and New – diverse as if assigned
to Faith and Doubt by a phrenologist,
this city which in winter light appears
unstable as a mirage, conjured north,
which vanishes in sleeves of autumn mist
or down perspectives to the Firth of Forth.

What spectral wynds I wandered through without you;
what wall-eyed tenements I made my own!
Doubting myself, I couldn't help but doubt you.
I'd glimpse you on a bridge against the sky,
always with other men. At night, alone,
I'd hear your rapid footfall in the rain.
In maudlin mood, I half wanted to die
to make you share, if not my love, my pain.

Edinburgh healed our year-long separation.
One slowly-fading evening of late spring
we found the ends of an old conversation
and held them along Candlemaker Row
to Victoria Street. There, I always bring
my dreaming to an end: like a tired child,
I stand where, on the steps to Upper Bow,
my cold heart thawed and we were reconciled.

Recycling

'Riddle me, riddle!', my father intones
as, entering my nightmares again,
in the suit of grey tweed that we buried him in,
he circles the square in the rain.

'You unearthed your old bicycle, then', I observe
as he pedals by, recklessly fast.
'I let it find me', he replies; 'all possessions
return to their owners at last'.

Then, suddenly close to my window, he adds,
averting his sockets from me:
'It's you, in the house of your fears, who are buried;
out here, in the weather, we're free'.

Branch Line

This early on a Saturday
our rural station seems
a gate through which to slip away
to the country of our dreams -

much as it seemed when, years ago,
we came to this small town,
with luggage and a child in tow
and plans to settle down.

A few weekenders clatter out
across the booking hall.
The train recedes and, in a rout
behind it, may-flowers fall

until, in that unfocussed light
that knows the sea is near
the empty line curves out of sight –
the line that brought us here.

It hangs like history, that thread,
self-spun, from which we dangle
and which connects us to the dead.
We journey from a tangle

of other lives – progenitors –
a spectral swirl of faces
dispersed on trade-winds or by wars –
who settled distant places

or who, as children, roused from bed
with only nightshirts on
through burning streets and squares were led
from Troy and Babylon.

Little Susie's Self-Portrait in a Garden
For Susie

Curled in a deckchair with a book,
like a worm in an apple, she adapts her surroundings,
to nourishment or defence:
lozenges of buddleia; lollipops of laburnum;
rampart of fir; moat of grass.
Beyond these, flourishes a profusion
of pencilled, shark's-tooth zig-zags,
too vaguely imagined for colour.
The sun is necessary, but too rude
to enter; just a quarter
of his round, unshaven face peers
from a corner of the paper. The lawn
is not my lawn, patchy, uneven: it is
a sacred space, daring entry,
a mystic lake at the plumb centre of which,
holding her book of spells, Susie
presides by the enchantment of
a minuscule 'u',
a smile, seen entire,
though her face is in profile,
a small hook,
baited for happiness.

Onshore

These days, in early autumn,
a restless sea-wind blows;
like some uncouth invader,
through wood and field it goes,
abating, softening, losing
the tang of wrack and sand
and, by degrees, acquiring
civility inland.

Incompleat Anglers

They stand, two young boys, on a bank,
each wielding a fishing-rod,
their father, whom they have to thank
for what must be their Christmas presents, noting
their efforts with a nod.

Several millennia have passed
since fish swam here; for now, the boys
have neither hook nor net, but cast
small weights across a meadow; yet they're not playing;
these presents are not toys.

They're friendly rivals, naturally;
but that the elder is no match
for his brother, even I can see;
the younger flicks his rod as if he merely
raised and dropped a latch.

No doubt, in years to come, he'll say
'My father taught me all I know'
and call to mind a winter day
when, dazzled by the frost and slanting sunlight,
he learnt to fish – although

I'd hesitate to call this 'teaching':
'conjuring', perhaps … They stand
like archetypes, these figures, reaching
forward and back – far back, to when fish swam
where there is now dry land.

The Small Street

On the small street, the back street,
someone washes a car,
someone plays a guitar
and the hole filled with rubble
is once more a puddle
where earth and sky meet.

On the small street, the back street,
the houses don't end;
they expand and extend,
put out lean-tos and sheds
and raise comfortable beds
for potatoes and beet.

And, of course, there are flowers
on the small street, the back street –
flowers geranious
and also spontaneous:
willowherb, bramble
and wild roses rambl-
ing, both dog- and sweet-.

Blessèd the child
brought up on this street:
wherever life take him
its birdsong will wake him
and, even in despair,
he'll know it's still there,
directing his feet.

II

In Senestan

A barren, isolated place
it was, the frontier. A bored sentry
surveyed each document and face
and allowed entry.

Gone now the squares, cafés and fountains,
the statues to the famous dead;
life here is simpler; those are mountains,
not clouds, ahead.

And yet it answers to a need,
this spareness. The plain was over-sexed.
Among these hills, if not quite freed,
we're less perplexed.

I mean, we're growing old, my dear,
and age defines itself by lack.
We've crossed that barely-marked frontier
and can't turn back.

Approaching the Magic Mountain
after Thomas Mann

They'd followed for a while the metalled road
beside the railway on the valley-floor;
but now, as if to emphasise their separation
from daily life, their licensed idleness,
their way diverged; they rode along a track
that crossed a brook and soon began to climb,
leading the little group toward the woods.
It seemed to rise suddenly above them;
how could they not have noticed it before:
the sanatorium, its tower and dome commanding
the promontory on which it stood, its walls
riddled by balconies, as if diseased?
Sunset faded; quite quickly, it grew dark.
Villages became small constellations
twinkling far below. Narrower tracks
wound like smoke among the pines. The mountains
hung in folds of indigo, admitting
a last chink of light on the horizon,
where the valley rose to a high pass and now
a breeze awoke that chilled them to the marrow.

Rose & Crown

Where the roof of mossy tiles sags down
to within three feet of the ground,
in the sun outside the Rose and Crown,
sound reaches me in layers: the chatter
of a crowd of regulars; the clatter
of knives and forks; the chink of glass;
a stream purling nearby; the breeze,
sifted by alder leaves and grass;
children's laughter from the swings
in an old orchard; and the sound
of wings, thousands of insect wings
shimmering in the air – all these
weave in my unfocussed ear
a glancing, auditory mist.
I could sit lost in it for hours –
here in this democratic garden
where weeds grow stalk by stalk with flowers
and where, after several rounds of beer,
my failings find a ready pardon
and failure ceases to exist.

Oxford

The years I spent here ought to make
the place familiar, but I feel lost;
I take a walk I used to take,
as strange to it as any ghost,

and fetch up in a small café.
Outside, the street is drenched with light;
bicycles tick the hours away –
the hours of youth, chilly and bright;

while, opposite the narrow room,
a horse-chestnut divests itself,
filling the gutters with drifts of bloom
from shelf on candle-laden shelf.

So many days, so soon …

Death in Lewes

She's dead.
Her children – neither hers nor children now –
for what will be the last time, occupy
the narrow house that is no longer home.
One daughter strips the bed,
the other raises the sash-window
and cups her hands to free a ragged moth.
Those papers (neatly tied) must be gone through,
those books donated to the Great Unread,
her grand piano, like a tragic hero,
borne reverently off stage,
and furniture, scarred veterans of her parties,
bestowed on charity;
but, for a while, these tasks postponed,
the sisters join her last few friends downstairs –
last frail threads in a broken web of friendship.
The sisters search for bottles and an opener.
Their brother sits in undistracted gloom:
'Those eco-undertakers she arranged
turned out to be two girls who couldn't lift her;
they had to drag her downstairs in a bag –
bio-degradable, no doubt.'
Tears track the wrinkles on his cheeks.
A sister sets a glass of wine beside him,
while, pausing for a moment, her elder sibling
gazes across the garden
and, in that moment, entertains a picture:
her mother's ragged soul,
free now to wing
above the trees in bud, the luminous rooftops,
into the empty brilliance of spring.

Zeteticism

Whatever savants say,
the world is flat, not round;
the ships that crowd the bay
are for its limit bound.

Their cargoes likewise, all
consigned to one address,
at death's great waterfall
plunge into nothingness.

The brightwork, the white sails
unfurled against the sky,
the million knots and nails
for such a voyage, why?

A Summer Pageant

Someone has left the bank unmown
and now, in June, the grass has grown
tall, thronged and pennanted with seed.
Threading the crowd, yellow hawkweed
thrusts out flowers like urchins' faces.
That pedlar to forgotten places,
lesser bindweed, untwists striped cones
of marzipan. Big as doubloons,
a slew of ox-eye daisies pays
for miniature firework displays
of clover (pink and white) and vetch.
Through the unkempt hedge above, stretch
the arched limbs of a rose, its blooms
like girls' faces in upstairs rooms.
That blue, unfocussed, poet's eye
is a first scabious. Across the sky,
a single banner of bright cloud drifts.
A sudden ecstasy of swifts
evanesces.
              Time-bound, I stand,
briefcase and mackintosh in hand,
and barely hear the traffic pass:
an ageing man beguiled by grass.

Trees

Calmer than the largest cetacean,
they swim through time, interweaving
the fleeting traces of our lives
with their perennial migration.
Though phonically composed of sighs,
their language has no term for grieving;
however rudely autumn drives
the gesturing spume of cloud, the trees
still promise peace – a peace that lies
just out of reach. It is as if
their streaming heads rose up to bless
not our present greed and strife,
but islands in unconsciousness,
those myths – or are they memories? –
that punctuate oblivion
when days, like crowded sails, are gone.

Light Aircraft
For Cris

Light aircraft in the summer sky
reminded you of holidays,
of playing in your father's gaze
beside a grove of pines. Nearby,

the Mediterranean gently breathed,
forbidden until, daily at four,
your family marched down to the shore,
towels rolled and beach-umbrella sheathed.

The shade in which you played alone
slowly lengthened; your little band
of dolls sipped coffee made from sand;
your father weighted, with the stone

you'd found for him, his pile of notes;
and the sun, which through closed shutters kept
a still watch where your mother slept,
silvered the tiny planes like motes.

The grove whispered of adulthood,
a kiss essayed, cigarette lipped,
a gate through which your siblings slipped
into the mysteries of the wood

and, in time, emerged to separate lives.
Now, last to call your life your own –
your parents gone, your children flown –
you see, from the multiple perspectives

that age allows, the half-closed ring
each generation forms, of love,
like an inlet viewed from high above,
its gaze requiting evening.

Poste Restante

Time chooses it eventually,
the place one settles down:
a village or a country town,
or somewhere by the sea.

And thus a spot one chanced upon
with no intent to stay
(not out of season, anyway,
with all the young folk gone)

becomes a mortal last address
at which one hopes to find
that solace of an ageing mind:
the peace of loneliness.

The Park at Dusk

The park renounces light
and starts to freeze;
it's already night
beneath the trees.

The winter sun that brought
long-shadowed people
tints, as an afterthought,
a distant steeple.

Sunset fades and now
a child's balloon,
released by a black bough,
becomes a moon –

a blanched moon that the pond
fails to reflect;
has cold unmade the bond
which should connect

artist and subject-matter?
Or can whatever
clear spirit dwells in water
grow weary, sever

relations with the world
and, faintly glowing,
sink, round its own thoughts curled,
toward unknowing?

Valediction

i.m. P.K.D.

His dying was, like all he did,
performed without self-pity.
In life, his story told, he'd bid
a brisk farewell and with his pack
and stick – a rustic in the city –
stride off and not look back.

For him, the race was to the swift;
stone urn and sculpted mourner
were worthless, neither prize nor gift.
He'd never sanction this, our last
detention of him at the twilit corner
he turns toward the past.

The Bell

It was as if a bell had tolled,
a bell of such great girth
it wasn't so much heard above
as felt beneath the earth;

and we, who'd never heard it, stood
astonished, wondering
what blind force hauling on what rope
in darkness made it swing.

The old had warned us; we, of course,
ignored them; we were young;
we thought they'd melted down the iron
and silenced the rough tongue.

But no; the bell was merely still.
It waited in its tower
until we broke the rusty lock
and re-awoke its power.

We know the bell; the bell knows us;
a new and bestial note
within us answers the command
issuing from its throat.

Sleep's Accomplice

Sleep and Sleep's accomplice called
and, reassured they'd cause no pain,
I held my dog while they injected
poison in his vein.

The poor beast merely seemed surprised;
he lay, unmoving, on his side;
then, as the numbness touched his heart,
whimpered once and died.

He was – my dog – lame, deaf, half-blind;
for months, his death had been discussed;
until my doubts were laid to rest
and I betrayed his trust.

Sleep and Sleep's accomplice zipped
the limp corpse in a bag. Through tears,
I watched them drive away with him,
my friend of fifteen years.

I glimpse him still, though rarely now,
a welcoming shadow in the hall,
or feel him nosing me awake
to offer me his ball.

Prodigal
Luke 15: 11-32

The old man must have kept his eyes on
the road for years, scanning the way
his son had gone to the horizon
of umber hills. Then came the day

when, shouting incoherently,
he shambled off to meet the lad;
the labourers, who didn't see
the distant figure, thought him mad.

The lost son had at last returned;
clean clothes were fetched; the maid drew water;
his hair was cut; his rags were burned;
the trusting calf was led to slaughter.

Others watch, year after year,
those same curves, snaking down the slope,
that never bring the lost one near,
and make a sacrifice of hope.

Evening Lights

Returning from the funeral,
I leave the motorway and take
a country road, for darkness' sake.
The hills that from a distance seemed
a black, impenetrable wall,
prove, as the narrow road ascends,
habitable – like grief. It ends
quietly, a day I only dreamed
would come. A blackbird calls somewhere
among the trees beside the road –
trees bent as if beneath a load
borne too long, too great to bear.
Night rises from the fields. The land
forgets itself. The travelling box
that shuts me in likewise grows dim.
I turn the headlamps on; they skim
bare hedges, walls of crumbling blocks
and ruts where scraps of water stand
and harden at the landscape's heart.
Far off, a few lit panes appear,
though walls and roofs are lost to sight.
Do people choose to live out here
or do they simply drift apart?
At last, the sky alone is light,
though colourless, a frozen lake
between the crests of hills that press
around my road in mourning dress.
Good Lord, what lonely ends we make.

Countryfolk
Luke 2:8-20

God knows what they're doing here,
these countryfolk, come down
in muddy boots and working gear
to our once-royal town.

They should be guarding sheep tonight
on snowy moors, instead
of troubling townsfolk with the sight
of hands that keep us fed.

Could they be revolutionaries
intent on causing harm?
Hardly! Why, one even carries
a lamb under his arm!

Their tread, though, as they pass the drunk,
who holds his nose and jeers,
and lodgings full to the last bunk,
is steady as the years.

They turn in at Old Adam's yard
and gather round the door
of the stable that was patched and tarred,
but never lit before.

There, one kneels, one stands, gnarled and thin,
tears streaking his tanned face,
and only the little lamb goes in
as if it knew the place.

Archipelago

Now that my sun is in the west,
the memory of my home town seems
to shine like islands of the blest
seen from the height of dreams.

An upstairs window blazes red;
a garden hoards the evening light;
two glistening roads diverge and head
downhill and out of sight.

My parent's house and my best friend's,
school, church and long-demolished station,
to these, my recollection lends
its false illumination.

Between the town, though, and those places
I'd aim for on long walks, a grey,
forgetful flood has washed the traces
of street and path away.

Goathurst Common, Gracious Lane,
Ivy Hatch and One Tree Hill,
Underriver, Mackerels Plain,
Seal Chart and Dibden Mill –

these fragments, freed from earthly maps,
acquire a supernatural glow,
like sacred shrines and groves, perhaps,
that only adepts know.

Or river-ice which, with the spring,
begins to sunder into floes –
like ice, once firm, now glittering
and melting as it goes.

Newly Arrived

It would, I imagine, be like setting out
from a foreign hotel as a spring day is dawning,
when air is champagne and there's no-one about,
to watch a new city emerge into morning.

The tops of glass towers are first to appear,
tinted pink by a sun that, no more than a sliver
of blinding vermilion, lifts itself clear
from the white scarf of mist still concealing the river.

Then the light touches church spires and trees in the park,
where chattering classes of starlings assemble,
joggers jog, flowers flower and pampered dogs bark.
A tram trundles by; electric threads tremble.

And, just as the pavement turns gold at one's feet
and one wonders where breakfast is served before seven,
a café proposes a window-side seat.
It would be like that, a first morning in heaven.

Notes

Waking in Weymouth
A painted statue of the 18th century monarch, George III, erected by the grateful citizens, surveys Weymouth Bay, where the king bathed in the hope of curing his incipient insanity. The king's visits made Weymouth a fashionable resort.

Camera Obscura
A camera obscura, literally a 'dark room', projected an image of the view before it onto a backdrop.

Endymion
Endymion was a shepherd-boy with whom Selene, Goddess of the Moon, fell in love. The last stanza refers to the darker patches on the moon, once thought to be seas, now known to be craters.

The Headland Cemetery
The poem is a version of Paul Valéry's masterpiece, *Le Cimitière Marin,* set in the cemetery above his native town, Cète, on the French Mediterranean coast.

Alice
Alice Liddell, daughter of the Dean of Christ Church, Oxford, was the girl to whom Lewis Carroll told the stories which became *Alice in Wonderland.* The sequel, *Through the Looking-Glass,* is based on moves in a game of chess in which Alice is a pawn, eventually promoted to queen.

Miss Butterfly
The title refers to Puccini's opera, *Madama Butterfly. Kanji* are Japanese ideograms; the strokes forming them are written in a prescribed order. The *Daimonji* is a hill above Kyoto.

Incompleat Anglers
The title refers to Izaak Walton's 17th century manual, *The Compleat Angler.*

Zeteticism is the belief that the earth is flat.

Valediction
The dedication is to the American poet, the late Peter Kane Dufault.

O, Little Town
The title refers to the Christmas hymn, O Little Town of Bethlehem, by Bishop Phillips Brooks.

Archipelago
The places named are all near Sevenoaks, Kent.